Penguin English
Introducing Applied Linguistics

Professor Ronald Carter has published extensively in the field of language and education and has written numerous articles and has edited books in the area of language learning and teaching, applied linguistics and in literary-linguistic studies. His main publications include: *Language and Literature: A Reader in Stylistics*; *Vocabulary: Applied Linguistic Perspectives*; and *Seeing through Language* with Walter Nash. He has been a member of the NCLE Standing Committee, particulary involved with language awareness schemes and has been a member of CNAA panels for Linguistics, Humanities and for Language and Literacy, as well as chairman of the Poetics and Linguistics Association of Great Britain. He is currently a member of the Literature Advisory Committee of the British Council. And since 1979 he has been in the Department of English Studies at the University of Nottingham where he teaches modern English language and literature, contemporary literature and cultural theory and educational linguistics.

Ronald Carter is Co-Editor of this series.

David Nunan is Associate Professor in Linguistics and Director of Research and Development at the National Centre for English Language Teaching and Research at Macquarie University, Sydney, Australia. He has worked as a TESOL teacher, teacher educator, curriculum designer, and materials writer and consultant in Britain and overseas and is the author of many books on applied linguistics and ELT.

Introducing

APPLIED

LINGUISTICS

AN A–Z GUIDE

Ronald Carter

Series Editors:
Ronald Carter and David Nunan

PENGUIN ENGLISH

PENGUIN ENGLISH

Published by the Penguin Group
Penguin Books Ltd, 27 Wrights Lane, London W8 5TZ, England
Penguin Books USA Inc., 375 Hudson Street, New York, New York 10014, USA
Penguin Books Australia Ltd, Ringwood, Victoria, Australia
Penguin Books Canada Ltd, 10 Alcorn Avenue, Toronto, Ontario, Canada M4V 3B2
Penguin Books (NZ) Ltd, 182–190 Wairau Road, Auckland 10, New Zealand

Penguin Books Ltd, Registered Offices: Harmondsworth, Middlesex, England

First published 1993
1 3 5 7 9 10 8 6 4 2

Typeset by Datix International Limited, Bungay, Suffolk
Set in 10/13 pt Lasercomp Times Roman
Printed by Clays Ltd, St Ives plc

Preface and Acknowledgements

The A–Z of applied linguistics is designed as an introduction to the field. Although the insights of linguistics are regularly applied to several other domains, the main emphasis in this book is on applications to first and to second or foreign language teaching.

Because of its introductory design, this book is not comprehensive (although a select bibliography suggests books for further study). In this respect, introductions are more difficult to write than more encyclopaedic guides for the selection of entries becomes an even more relative and subjective task. In this enterprise, I am grateful for the advice, assistance and critical comments I have received from colleagues, teachers (both EFL / ESL and English as a Mother Tongue), and from students and student teachers following pre-service and in-service courses in applied linguistics. Particular thanks are due to my co-editor of this series, David Nunan, and to Mike McCarthy. I am also grateful to John Harris and Jeff Wilkinson for being able to draw on a draft glossary which we wrote for the LINC (Language in the National Curriculum) project. The essentially problem-solving view of applied linguistics adopted by that project has also provided a framework for focusing on areas of language learning and teaching which linguists and teachers can address jointly and collaboratively. Such a view sets an agenda which is neither wholly the teacher's nor wholly the linguist's agenda and is thus, it is hoped, particularly appropriate to an introductory guide.

Ronald A. Carter
Department of English Studies, University of Nottingham
1 October 1992

accent   Those features of pronunciation which identify a person either geographically or socially.

A geographical accent can be associated with a specific town or city (e.g. Liverpool, New York) or a particular region (e.g. Texas) or with national groups speaking the same language (e.g. Australian). It can also show whether a speaker is a native speaker of a language. For example, 'She speaks French with an English accent.'

Social accents relate more to social and educational background. An example of this in Britain is **Received Pronunciation (RP)**, commonly known as 'BBC English', 'posh', or 'Oxford English'. This is a geographically neutral accent often associated with public schools and professional uses. Because of its geographical neutrality, it is popularly but wrongly thought that people speaking in RP have no accent. In terms of a linguistic description of accent, everyone has an accent, which may be geographical or social or both and vary according to the speaker's situation.

RP is the model of pronunciation which figures prominently in courses for the teaching of English as a foreign or second language and is the preferred model in a number of countries overseas. Increasingly, however, the model is seen as simply one of many national accents, and other native-speaker accents, such as Australian and American English, are being taught in contexts where it had previously been assumed that there was only one correct form of pronunciation. The choice of pronunciation model, as well as the variety of international English taught, is also an ideological choice. Language learners in several countries pride themselves on the greater sense of national identity conferred by speaking English with an Indian or a Nigerian or a Singaporean accent. (see also **dialect; pronunciation**)

accuracy   (see **fluency**)

acquisition (of language)   In some theories, language acquisition is opposed to language learning. Acquisition is seen as a more natural process which has parallels with first language development. Acquisition results from meaningful exposure to naturally occurring language and from using it for meaningful communication. Language acquisition results from unconscious and intuitive responses to language. It contrasts with processes of language learning in which explicit knowledge about the forms of a language is presented more regularly for conscious learning. (see also **Natural Order Hypothesis**)

action research   Action research refers to the investigations into successful language learning undertaken by teachers in their own classrooms. Action research can be individual and collaborative but it is more likely to be valuable and stimulating when the questions explored are those posed by teachers themselves. It is an important principle of modern teacher development that the best and most reflective teachers are often also active researchers in their own classroom.

active / passive knowledge of language   An active knowledge of language is demonstrated when language learners actively *produce* their own spoken or written texts. A passive knowledge of language is harder to demonstrate or assess, but it is the capacity of a language learner to *understand* the language produced by others. Most language users understand more language than they actually produce themselves. This is particularly so in the case of vocabulary. For example, our passive or receptive vocabulary will necessarily be greater than our active or productive vocabulary.

affective filter   Affective filter is a term used to describe the way in which a learner's disposition or state of mind can influence the way in which language is received. Anxious learners have a high affective filter. They lack confidence, they become embarrassed by direct contact with the target language and are fearful of making mistakes. A low affective filter is necessary for successful language learning. In order to lower the affective filter, research has demonstrated that language work should focus on meaningful communication, on fluency rather than accuracy, and should take place in a relaxed, enjoyable, activity-centred classroom atmosphere. Also important is a wide exposure to vocabulary, which learners will value because they can use it for making personal meanings. Such a classroom context produces well-motivated learners with positive attitudes towards language learning. Such learners will normally have a low affective filter.

affective filtering This is a term used for a process by which learners model their language according to a particular variety of the target language (for example, native speakers, a peer group, family, a teacher, and so on).

AILA AILA stands for Association Internationale de Linguistique Appliquée – an international association for the study of applied linguistics.

applied linguistics As this book illustrates, applied linguistics is the application of linguistic theories, descriptions and methods to the solution of language problems which have arisen in a range of human, cultural and social contexts. One of the main contexts for its application is the exploration of problems in language learning and teaching and, for many, the term is used with almost exclusive reference to this field. However, the term applied linguistics is used in relation to other fields, such as: literary studies (**stylistics**); **translation studies**; **lexicography**; **language planning**; as well as specific branches of linguistics such as **clinical linguistics** and **critical linguistics**. Ideally, applied linguists should work alongside other professionals in the exploration of language problems or difficulties so that the application of linguistics becomes the result of a genuine synthesis rather than one in which answers are found only according to an agenda provided by the linguist.

assessment   (see **testing / tests**)

audio-lingual method   This is a method for the teaching of a foreign language. It is also known as the aural–oral method. It derives from the techniques of intensive foreign language instruction developed for teaching American military personnel during the Second World War. The method is said to result in rapid acquisition of speaking and listening skills. It has some similarities to the **Direct Method** of language teaching and is based on the following main principles: speaking and listening competence precedes competence in reading and writing; use of the mother-tongue is discouraged in the classroom; language skills are a matter of habit formulation, and great emphasis is therefore placed on practice of particular patterns of language through structured dialogues and **drills** until the use of language is sufficiently rehearsed for responses to be automatic.

The approach still enjoys popularity though it is criticized for its basis in behaviourism. Critics say that learners become restricted in expression and can lack the confidence to create new expressions for themselves.

bi-dialectalism   This refers to the ability of any one person to use two dialects of any one language. This principle is particularly important in relation to current debates on Standard English in schools. The National Curriculum in England and Wales requires that pupils be introduced to Standard Spoken and Standard Written English to give pupils a greater control over dialectal variety in relation to audience and purpose as well as an ability to communicate with a wider audience.

Bilingual Syntax Measure The Bilingual Syntax Measure (BSM) is a collection of pictures, in the form of cartoons, which are used to prompt language learners into using a particular sequence of morphemes. Thus, a picture showing people walking might form the basis of questions which elicited the use of the morpheme -*ed* to form the past tense (*walked*). Students are said to have acquired the syntactic structure if they used it correctly in 90 per cent of instances. The BSM has been criticized by several leading applied linguists on the grounds that it is arbitrary, restricted and context-bound in practice. It is argued that several measures are needed before accurate evidence can be provided of developmental processes in language.

bilingualism A bilingual is a person who has mastered the essential skills of writing, reading and speaking in two languages, although in most cases one language is known better than the other. It is also likely that the two languages will be used in different situations; for example, one language might be used at work, while the other might be used in the home. Bilinguals also code-switch between languages according to whom they are talking, according to the subject matter and according to the relative formality of the situation. Not all bilinguals are bicultural; that is, they may be able to speak two languages but may only know how to behave according to the values of the communities associated with one of the languages. (see also **code**; **culture**; **multilingualism**)

Black English Black English is the variety of language used by some Black British or Black Americans (the latter is also referred to as BEV or Black English Vernacular). Black British and Black American English have their own distinctive grammars and have been shown to be rule-governed languages in their own right. Much research into these languages has been in educational contexts and the research has done much to help teachers better understand the values attached by school children to the different languages and to understand the uses of Black English Vernacular and Standard American or British English according to the context and purpose of the communication.

bottom–up (processing)   According to bottom–up views, successful decoding of language is a matter of processing the smallest units of language first and then moving up to larger units of meaning. Thus, a bottom–up view of teaching listening comprehension focuses first on individual constituent sounds, then on words, and then on how the words are chained into sentences. A bottom–up approach to the teaching of reading would process language by moving from a discrimination of every letter to the matching of phonemes and graphemes (see **phonics**) to an eventual concern with reading groups of words and sentences for their overall meaning. Bottom–up approaches contrast with top–down views of language processing which focus on discoursal and real world knowledge as starting points for the decoding of meaning. Thus, a top–down view suggests that the reader or writer or listener is at the heart of the interpretation of language. It emphasizes active reconstruction of whole meanings rather than the simple decoding of form. Top–down approaches recognize the ways in which we form hypotheses and predictions about the way a text will develop, revising these hypotheses or seeing them confirmed as we proceed. Central to the process is an interaction of the reader (or listener), their experience and knowledge (see **schema theory**), and the language of a text, spoken or written. Several contemporary approaches underline that it is important for teachers to combine top–down and bottom–up procedures.

CALL   CALL stands for Computer Assisted Language Learning. As its name suggests, it refers to the use of computers in the language classroom. An increasing number of computer programs are now available which support language learning at most stages of development.

caretaker language This term is a collective term for the language used by parents, babysitters and other adults generally when they talk to children. The term 'motherese' is also used since interactions between mothers and babies and young children are highly regular in most societies. Caretaker language is characterized by shorter utterances, simpler grammatical structures, exaggerated speech patterns, and by lots of repetition. Such language use contains some universal features but there are also interesting contrasts based on culture, gender and age differences.

chronological text (see **genre**)

clinical linguistics A branch of applied linguistics in which methods and theories of linguistics are applied to an analysis of language handicaps such as spoken and written disorders or to an understanding of sign languages for the deaf. (see also **LARSP**)

CLL (see **Community Language Learning**)

COBUILD COBUILD is an abbreviation for Collins Birmingham University International Language Database. The database is a collection of naturally occurring spoken and written texts, initially over twenty million words but now totalling many millions more. The COBUILD project is a computer-assisted project designed to provide accurate linguistic information to support the design of pedagogic materials such as dictionaries, grammars and course books. (see also **dictionary**; **naturalness**)

coda (see **genre**)

code This is a term which is sometimes used in place of terms like dialect, or language variety. It can also be used as a synonym for language itself. In the work of the British sociologist, Basil Bernstein, the term code has a further, more specialist meaning.

For Bernstein, a distinction needs to be drawn between an **elaborated code** and a **restricted code**. Restricted codes arise between speakers who share similar assumptions and understandings. The language is embedded in specific contexts and contains forms of language such as pronouns and tag questions which leave meanings implicit. By contrast, elaborated codes are more explicit and they arise where the social relations between speakers are more formal and less taken for granted. Some have argued from these distinctions that middle-class children have access to both codes, whereas working-class children are more likely to be limited to a restricted code and to experience difficulty in acquiring the more complex, elaborate and explicit forms of language required, for example, by schools. The theory has, however, been controversial and researchers have misinterpreted the theory as demonstrating that working-class children lack, for example, powers of abstract thought.

A more widely used term in the context of language teaching is **code-switching**. This refers to the decisions made by speakers to select one language or one variety of language according to the purpose, social context or audience for language use. Code-switching can even sometimes occur in the middle of a dialogue or sentence. For example, in Singapore, a Chinese speaker might use Cantonese at home, Mandarin Chinese at work, Singapore English between friends, and Malay to Indians or Malays at the local market. (see also **bi-dialectalism**)

code-switching   (see **code**)

cognitive code learning   Cognitive code learning developed at a time when **audio-lingual methods** were prominent. Unlike audio-lingualism, however, cognitive code learning places less emphasis on memorization and there is greater acceptance that mistakes can be an important part of the language learning process. Cognitivism values rules but the emphasis is on language learning as an active problem-solving process with learners guided towards their own understanding of the rules. Rote learning and drilling of rules is consequently de-emphasized. The role of the teacher is to stimulate a learner's mental activity and to provide classroom contexts which assist learners to relate new language knowledge to existing knowledge.

coherence   For a text to be fully satisfactory to a listener or reader, it needs not only appropriate grammatical links between sentences (**cohesion**) but it also needs the concepts, propositions or events to be related to each other and to be consistent with the overall subject of the text. This semantic and propositional organization is called coherence. (see **schema theory**)

cohesion   Two major means can be identified by which a series of sentences or utterances cohere to create a meaningful text. **Coherence** refers to the underlying semantic unity by which the reader or listener perceives that propositions, actions or events fit together. Cohesion refers to the grammatical means by which the elements are linked, usually at sentence level. The most common forms of grammatical connection are:

1 reference by the use of:

- personal pronouns, such as *she, he, they, it*, referring to a preceding full lexical noun (e.g. *The woman crossed the road. She was wearing a blue scarf.*)
- the definite article, *the* (e.g. *It was raining. The rain was cold.*)
- deictics, such *this, that, these, those* (e.g. *There are two sets of books. I'll take these.*)
- comparative forms, such as *other* (e.g. *There were two men. One was young. The other was middle-aged.*)

2 substitution by the use of pro-forms, such as *do, so, one(s)*, which stand in for full lexical words or phrases (e.g. *Most children like chocolate. Some adults do too.*)

Cohesion is also created by the use of linking words. Conjunctions are the most immediately recognizable. The three main types are:

1 temporal – *then, previously, later*
2 additive – *moreover, And* (in initial position)
3 causal / result – *but, however*

Lexical chaining, that is a sequence of identical or closely related words, can also create a strong sense of cohesion provided that there is also a semantic unity underlying the text. (see **discourse analysis; vocabulary**)

collaborative learning The theory and practice of collaborative learning underlines that we can learn from each other as well as from a teacher and that one of the most important tasks of the teacher is to create sufficient classroom opportunities for such learning to take place. Opponents of collaborative learning tend to see such practices as unstructured and inefficient but supporters see benefits in children working together to solve problems, to share ideas and perceptions, and to produce work which draws on the strengths of a group and which will therefore be of enhanced quality. The active involvement of collaborative work is said to be both motivating and stimulating to those involved and to teach the values of mutual support and teamwork. Collaborative learning can extend to pupils correcting and commenting on each other's work.

Collaborative learning is practised across the language curriculum and is especially well-rehearsed in processes of talk and, increasingly, in writing development where an alternative widely used term is **conferencing**. Its successes depend at all times on careful planning and monitoring by the teacher at all stages.

Applied linguistics can be of relevance to teachers' understanding of collaborative learning. For example, in exploring the kinds of processes which underly collaborative writing tasks, an analysis of different stages in the linguistic shaping of a text can be of value to teachers, in guiding the kind of interventions they make and the kind of support they give to their students' use of language.

communicative approach   This is an approach to foreign language teaching which emphasizes the learner's ability to use the language appropriately in specific situations. Considerable importance is given in this approach to the functions of language and to helping learners become communicatively competent, by knowing which language to select for particular purposes. The communicative approach aims to teach an ability not simply to use the language in grammatically correct sentences but also to know when, where and to whom to use such language.

The communicative approach developed as a reaction against **grammar–translation** and **audio-lingual method**s which did not sufficiently stress the communicative uses of the language. It built on the **notional–functional syllabus** which organizes teaching units according to the communicative 'notions' a learner requires in order to communicate successfully.

The communicative approach has been developed mainly by British applied linguists and has been influential on syllabus design and on teaching methods in many parts of the world. It continues to be developed as teachers experience the approach in practice and explore ways of refining communicative methodologies. Such methodologies stress the processes of communication and aim to engage learners actively in tasks such as problem solving, information retrieval, and social exchanges. One of the main challenges for the communicative approach is to interrelate the functions of language with the correct use of structures, that is, to combine communicative fluency with formal accuracy.

Community Language Learning   Community Language Learning is an approach to teaching and learning languages developed by Charles Curran. It is an essentially humanistic theory of second or foreign language learning. It stresses the development of the kind of 'whole person' relationship found in counselling therapy. The method makes use of group learning in both small and large groups, the groups acting as the 'community'. A main aim is to remove as much as possible of what might be found threatening in the language learning situation. Indeed, the students can use their first language to express personal feelings and attitudes and the teacher (known as the 'counsellor') will help them to find equivalent expressions in the target language. The learner will then repeat these expressions to other members of the group. The teacher does not normally prepare material in advance.

complicating action   (see **genre**)

conferencing   Conferencing is a term, used particularly in connection with the teaching of writing, which refers to a process of consultation between teacher and pupil. During this process, the teacher provides advice and guidance to the pupil, usually at significant points in the writing of drafts. The degree of intervention, the decision whether to focus on language or on content, the extent to which pupils consult with one another as well as with the teacher, will depend on the teacher's own view of what constitutes successful learning at particular points in the process.

consciousness-raising (CR)   This is a process by means of which learners are made more aware of the structure of a target language. Consciousness-raising, like **KAL** and **language awareness**, aims to create more effective language learning environments by making conscious knowledge about language an integral part of the process of language learning. A common practice is to provide learners with appropriate tasks which stimulate comparison between the structures of the target language and the structures of the learner's own language. Advocates of consciousness-raising do not propose the use of drills or the teaching of structure out of context (see **drills**; **grammar–translation method**); neither do they propose unconscious immersion in a language of the extreme kind supported by some advocates of communicative language teaching. Rather, an integrated and balanced attention to both form and use is endorsed.

context Context is a complex notion because it concerns not only features of the external, non-linguistic environment in which a text is composed and interpreted, but also the internal, linguistic environment of the text itself. The features of these two environments interplay in the production and comprehension of both spoken and written texts and are consequently important for any language learner.

The main features of the external context can be identified through asking four questions:

1 *Who are the participants (writer/speaker, reader/listener) involved in the communicative event?* Recognition of the audience is a very important factor in any interaction since it governs the nature of the text produced. If, for example, students fail to recognize their audience, then the text they produce could be either too informal or too complex. A letter, for instance, written to the editor of a newspaper will be different from a letter written to a friend; a legal document written for a lawyer differs from one addressed to the general public.

2 *Where is the communicative event taking place?* Participants need to focus on the actual location in which the text is produced and interpreted. Different settings will affect the nature of the communication. For instance, students talking

to each other in a play area will converse differently when they are in a classroom situation.

3 *Why is the communicative event taking place?* This question addresses the purpose of the written/spoken text: whether it aims to, for instance, inform, persuade or instruct.

4 *When is the communicative event taking place?* Writer/speakers and reader/listeners should take into account the time of both the composition and interpretation of a text.

It is difficult in the classroom situation to create an authentic external context. Frequently, contextual features are neither specified in tasks set nor considered in the discussion of a task. Students therefore often write for a non-specified audience and so typically focus on the teacher/examiner or else they ignore their reader altogether.

The internal environment of the text is also an established context, although not such an obvious one. All textual features whether at word, clause, or between-sentence level are part of an environment: any word relates to those words which surround it both in the immediate vicinity and in other parts of the text. Even whole texts are governed by their textual environment. Magazine advertisements, for example, will vary depending on the type of magazine.

By making students aware of the different features of context they should begin to recognize that any alteration of contextual features, whether internal to the text or external, will affect the nature of the communication.

contrastive hypothesis (contrastive analysis) The contrastive hypothesis states that a language learner's first language will have a crucial influence on the learning of a second language. Most obviously, errors made in the process of learning the second language will bear significant traces of interference from the first language. The hypothesis also states that learners' difficulties can be analysed, even predicted in advance, by a systematic contrastive comparison of the two languages involved. As a result of linguistic differences between languages, learners from different language backgrounds will, it is claimed, learn aspects of the target language in a different order. Not all the hypotheses of contrastivists are upheld, however, although there is recognized to be considerable value in contrastive analysis of the relevant languages by both learner and teacher. (see **interlanguage**)

contrastive rhetoric   Contrastive rhetoric is a study of how styles of writing and text structure vary from one culture to another. It is related to **contrastive analysis** (see **contrastive hypothesis**). The main aim is to assist students learning the conventions of academic discourse who transfer to their writing assumptions about argumentation, presentation of data and logical relations which are specific to their own culture but which do not apply in the text conventions of the target language. For example, some major Japanese rhetorical styles are characterized by abrupt transitions, by conclusions, or by attention to points which appear to be only vaguely related to a main topic. The structure depends on different cultural definitions of logic and relevance. Contrastive rhetoric studies are particularly useful in teaching contexts in which learners come from societies with marked differences in culture, ideology and belief systems.

conversational analysis   This approach to the description of language looks at conversational English from a mainly sociolinguistic perspective.

For example, the approach explores the notion of 'shared knowledge' as an aspect of conversation that can be identified as 'rule-governed' behaviour. Analysts, such as William Labov, state that all events that are reported in a two-way conversation can be seen as:

1 A events (i.e., those events known only to speaker A)
2 B events (i.e., those events known only to speaker B)
3 AB events (i.e., those events known both to A and B)

In an analysis of Harold Pinter's short drama sketch, *Last to Go*, this framework is used to identify how the conversation between the newspaper-seller and the coffee-stall holder is operated. Why is it like real conversation and why is it funny?

It is concluded that, in terms of real conversation, we all usually start talking to each other with AB events:

Person A: *Hello. How are you?*
Person B: *Fine, thanks. It's a nice day, isn't it?*
Person A: *Not as good as yesterday though.*

This structure appears in Pinter's sketch as well, but what makes the sketch humorous is that the participants are most of the time just continually confirming and questioning events they both already know:

Man: *You was a bit busy earlier.*
Barman: *Ah.*
Man: *Round about ten.*
Barman: *Ten, was it?*
Man: *About ten.*

Conversational analysis has much to offer the teacher:

- in terms of providing a possible framework for analysing talk in the classroom
- in providing the basis for a stylistic description of the language of drama texts.

(see also **genre**; **stylistics**; **text**)

creoles A creole is a pidgin which has become the mother-tongue of a community and which is used for many of the everyday communicative needs of speakers within that community.

Pidgins are the auxiliary languages in a community; they are learned alongside the main languages and used for such purposes as trading between people who do not share a common language. A pidgin is not a native language for any speaker.

Pidgins have a limited range of functions. The sentence structure and range of vocabulary of most pidgins are also restricted. Most pidgins do not last long. They disappear when different peoples no longer have a need for them (for example, trading contacts cease). Most pidgins are based on European languages such as English, French, Dutch and Portuguese, which reflect the colonial contexts in which they arose.

Pidgins commonly develop into creoles. This process, known as creolization, results in an expanded vocabulary and a more complex grammar. Creoles usually co-exist alongside the standard language from which they derive with speakers needing to code-switch between the two languages. Contrary to the popular stereotype, creoles are not inferior means of communication but are highly developed languages in their own right.

Pidgins and creoles are of interest to applied linguists for two main reasons. First, teachers may find themselves teaching in communities in which code-switching between creole and standard languages is common. An understanding of the nature of creoles and of the relationship between pidgins and creoles is important. Second, study of processes of creolization can reveal much about the development of languages from more simple to more complex forms. This can be of relevance for understanding processes of development in a second or foreign language.

critical linguistics   This is a relatively new field. It starts from the premise that systems and uses of language are not neutral. The emphasis is on using linguistic analysis to expose the ideologies which inform all spoken and written texts. There is a particular emphasis on the unmasking of ideologies in public and media discourse. For example, by comparing the following two headlines:

1 *IBM closes factory. Workers protest.*
2 *Workers attack closure of factory.*

critical linguists would point out how, in headline 1, greater responsibility is assigned to the company. In the second headline, 'workers' are fronted to a main subject position, are engaged in a transitive act of attacking and the change of the verb *close* into a noun *closure* allows all reference to the company to be removed. In the context of language teaching, critical linguists are interested in exposing the political and ideological contexts within which all language teaching practices take place.

cues The notion of grapho-phonic, syntactic and semantic cues applies to the concept of miscue analysis. This form of analysis represents a significant development in the assessment of reading in recent years. It involves children reading out a text aloud whilst an adult makes notes on a second copy of the text, paying special attention to deviations from the actual text.

Miscue, as a term, was coined by Kenneth Goodman, because for him it more satisfactorily represented a child's attempts to make sense of any text than the term 'mistake'.

Miscue analysis, therefore, has an important diagnostic function; and cues are graded along three dimensions:

1 grapho-phonic cues – sound/symbol relationships
2 syntactic cues – grammatical expectation
3 semantic cues – expectation of meaning

Given the danger of relying on the evidence of an oral reading of an unprepared text, such cues might well, at different levels of language comprehension, give the teacher insights into:

- consistent patterns of miscue
- what positive strategies for decoding a pupil is using
- what supports are available for interpreting meaning
- how the pupil might be helped to become a more efficient reader.

culture Culture is best defined as a set of beliefs and values which are prevalent within a society or section of a society. In some definitions, the term culture is reserved for the most prestigious achievements of a society. More generally, however, culture embraces the habits, customs, social behaviour, knowledge and assumptions associated with a group of people. The cultural forms of that group are the artefacts and texts, spoken and written, which represent the beliefs and values of a community.

Programmes of multicultural education are designed to acquaint students or pupils in school with cultures which are different from their own and which are often the cultures of other groups of people in the society in which they live. Most second or foreign language teaching involves learning something of the culture connected with the target language; indeed, in some traditions of language teaching (see the **grammar–translation method**) studying the canonical literature and cultural forms of the society's language is one of the main purposes.

The term 'acculturation' is also in use. It refers to the processes by which cultural changes occur in the beliefs and values of one group of people as a result of interaction with the beliefs and values of another group. Language is central to processes of acculturation. It should also be noted here how successful language learning may depend on the extent to which learners identify with the culture of the target language. In a related way, some learners may not learn effectively because the teaching methods employed (e.g. the teacher as counsellor; group work) conflict with their own cultural norms (e.g. teacher as didact).

Sometimes the terms cultural deprivation, cultural deficit or cultural disadvantage are used in the context of language education to refer to the fact that some children may not have cultural experiences (such as regular contact with books; conversations with sympathetic adults) which can be of value to them in school. It is important to recognize in this context, however, that there are relatively few universal cultural values and that no one set of cultural practices is inherently superior. Accordingly, it is important to ensure that language curricula and, especially, languages tests are 'culture-free' in so far as they do not disadvantage any particular cultural groups.

curriculum   A curriculum is broader in scope than a **syllabus**. It states the kinds of learning experiences, methodologies, underlying theories of learning and testing procedures which will enable learners to attain specific learning objectives.

deficit hypothesis   This is a theory that some children may lack certain codes of language that are needed for success in school. It contrasts with a **difference hypothesis** which states that all codes and dialects are equally complex and are equally able to be used for expressing ideas, feelings, etc. (see **code**; **culture**; **dialect**)

descriptive   (see **prescriptive**)

descriptive grammar   (see **grammar**)

dialect   This refers to a variety of the language that is identified geographically or socially by certain vocabulary or grammatical features, e.g. in the West Midlands of England – *Her's saft* (the word *saft* is a combination of *soft* and *daft*; and *her* is used here where other dialects would use *she*). Spoken forms of a dialect often become associated with a distinctive pronunciation (an **accent**). The dialect that now predominates, especially in writing, is called **Standard English**. There are different versions of Standard English, e.g. Standard British English, Standard American English, though grammatical and lexical differences between them are minor.

dictionary   The last decade has seen considerable advances in foreign-language lexicography which have resulted in a renewed interest in the relevance of dictionaries to processes of language learning. Dictionaries have been improved or developed with the needs of the language learner uppermost. There has been an extensive debate about the merits of examples made up by an experienced team of lexicographers and examples selected from a computer-based corpus of naturally occurring English. Proponents of made-up examples argue that such examples are more controlled and can be especially written to explain key aspects of grammatical or lexical use. Proponents of naturally occurring examples argue that such procedures result in artificial language and that a properly prepared corpus can illustrate how the language works by means of real examples. Real examples make the process of learning more natural and less contrived. (see **COBUILD**; **naturalness**)

difference hypothesis   (see **deficit hypothesis**)

diglossia   This is a term used to describe any situation where two different varieties of language exist in one speech community. Both varieties are felt to have equal status and are used by speakers as alternatives although usually one variety has a formal style and the other an informal style.

Direct Method   The Direct Method is an approach to the teaching of foreign languages. It developed in the late nineteenth century as a reaction against the **grammar–translation method**. In this method only the target language should be used in class and the learner should be at all times actively involved in using the language in realistic everyday situations. Students are encouraged to think in the foreign language and not translate in and out of it. Reading and writing are only taught after extensive speaking skills have been developed. Meanings are taught 'directly' through concrete vocabulary, and demonstration by the teacher, using gestures, mime, direct actions, and pictures. Communication skills are developed in small classes with the teacher organizing activities in a graded, progressive way and making much use of question–answer exchanges. In the Direct Method, grammar is normally only taught inductively. There is little emphasis on deductive teaching of the rules of language structure. There is more emphasis on fluency than on accuracy.

The principles of the Direct Method have been enthusiastically supported in many parts of the world, even though it is accepted that they are not easy to follow to the letter, in the artificial environment of the school language classroom.

discourse   This is a term used in a variety of different ways for a variety of different purposes. In this context, it would seem useful to identify five uses of the term.

1 The dictionary defines discourse as 'a serious talk or piece of writing which is intended to teach or explain something' (*Collins COBUILD English Language Dictionary*). In fact, in its verb form, *to discourse*, the meaning relates exclusively to speech – 'to talk in an authoritative way' – sometimes having pejorative associations of 'at length'.

2 It is also used, in a broader semiological sense, to refer to the topics and types of language used in specific contexts (*the discourse of Thatcherism, the discourse of high finance*).

3 Some linguists use discourse in a loose way to distinguish speech from writing. Discourse is used when talking about speech; whereas **text** is used when discussing writing.

4 Another perspective is the one that regards discourse as **process** and text as **product**.

5 Finally, the term 'discourse' is used in a much more general sense to refer to any naturally occurring stretch of language, spoken or written. In parallel, the term 'text' is also taking on this same meaning.

(see **discourse analysis**)

discourse analysis This is a relatively new discipline, which attempts to identify and describe linguistic regularities and irregularities in utterances which cannot be accounted for at a grammatical level (i.e., they operate above sentence level).

For example, the following two texts (the first spoken, the second written) contain no grammatical irregularities, but seem distinctly 'odd':

1 Teacher: *What is the capital of Outer Mongolia?*
   Pupil: *Yes, I'll do that for you.*
2 Once upon a time there lived a small green frog called Freda. Such creatures do not normally live long in captivity.

The analysis of discourse, is, therefore, the analysis of language *in use* across sentence boundaries and aims to create descriptive frameworks which try to account for how such texts are organized.

There have been several attempts recently to describe the nature of spoken language interchange. For example, researchers at the University of Birmingham, basing their description on an analysis of teacher/pupil talk in the classroom, established a basic notion of exchange structure where the typical conversational interaction between teacher and pupil consists of the following structure:

1 initiation   (mainly teacher-led)
2 response   (mainly pupil reply)
3 feedback   (mainly teacher 'evaluation')

An example would be:

Teacher: *Can you tell me why you eat all that food?* (initiation)
Pupil: *To keep you strong.* (response)
Teacher: *To keep you strong. Yes. To keep you strong.* (feedback)

It is important to note that such analysis is not essentially interested in such structures from an educational viewpoint. They are mainly concerned to provide a model of discourse which will be appropriate for all conversational interaction. It is significant, however, that the exchange structure most often produced in a classroom context seems to occur elsewhere only in a limited way, for example, in interviews, legal exchanges and doctor–patient interviews.

In longitudinal research into Bristol children talking at home and at school, researchers have developed a description of conversational interaction between adult and pupil and teacher and pupil from similar perspectives. Main conclusions are that:

- children need to be *actively* involved in their own learning
- it is the role of the adult to be guider, supporter and encourager.

It will be clear from these examples that results of the analysis of spoken discourse can be of value to teachers and that, in general, discourse analysis is properly concerned with the study and interpretation of the relationship between language and the contexts in which it is used.

Discourse analysis of written text is also a rapidly developing field of investigation. The areas of study here are also valuable to teachers in so far as methods and results of analysis can enable them to identify strengths and weaknesses in their students' construction of long stretches of written language.

For example, the following text lacks both coherence and relevant cohesive properties:

> The giant ant is very, very big. All the children run away and the dogs grumble. And we stare at t.v. all the houses fall down. Its eyes are large and beamey. Paul and I get on our bikes and ride fast, the blue and cream buses colaps with the big ant.

Analysis of this piece of written discourse reveals an inconsistent use of pronouns, an absence of a continuing chain of lexical words, constantly switching subjects and the introduction of new information which is not adequately contextualized for the reader. Though in some respects there is an imaginative use of language, the text does not 'hang together'. It is the task of written discourse analysis to explain the principles by which texts are organized across units of language larger than a single clause or sentence.

drills Language drills bring together a concern for structural analysis of the language and behaviourist theories that language is a matter of habit formation and that it is best learned through practice of particular patterns or structures of language. Drills are exercises which reinforce a learner's knowledge of particular patterns of language. For example, a substitution drill inserts a different word in a particular slot in order to practise a basic structure and basic associated vocabulary:

The	book	is	on	the	table.
The	pencil	is	by	the	desk.
The	pen	is	under	...	chair.

And so on.

EAP This is an abbreviation for English for Academic Purposes. (see **ESP**)

educational linguistics The term educational linguistics is often employed as a parallel term to applied linguistics. However, applied linguistics tends to be used to describe applications of linguistics to second or foreign language learning and teaching whereas educational linguistics is more frequently used in relation to first language learning and teaching. Although the main applications of linguistics are to educational contexts, as this book illustrates, the field of **applied linguistics** is much broader and more comprehensive than this.

EFL EFL is an abbreviation for English as a Foreign Language. English is learned as a foreign language in countries where it is a subject in schools but is *not* a medium of instruction *nor* the normal language of business, law and government, *nor* normally a language of everyday communication. In such countries, the mother-tongue of the people has an institutionalized role. Countries in which English is taught as a foreign language include Japan, Germany, France, Turkey, Brazil. (see **ESL**)

EIL An abbreviation for English as an International Language. EIL is the English used for purposes of international communication. Although such English will normally be modelled on native speaker varieties (such as Australian English or American English or British English), it can be spoken with any accent and will vary according to the contexts in which and purposes for which it is used. (see **dialect**; **Standard English**)

elaborated code   (see **code**)

ELT An abbreviation for English Language Teaching. The term is widely in use in Great Britain and in parts of the world influenced by British approaches to second and foreign language teaching. In North America and in parts of the world influenced by American approaches, the preferred term is normally **TESOL** (Teaching English to Speakers of Other Languages).

error (error analysis) All teachers and learners of a second language have to deal at some time with the question of errors. There may be many sources to the error and many different kinds of error. Several errors result from wrong deductions about the nature of the second language, for example, believing a pattern to conform to a general rule when it is an exception or when it is the result of an analogy with the mother-tongue. It has been claimed that regular **contrastive analysis** by the learner and, where possible, by the teacher can help overcome the most serious errors.

However, the analysis of errors is a complex matter and not all errors are internal to the language system. They may be due to external factors such as inadequate teaching or poorly prepared materials. Some errors may in certain contexts even be encouraged by teachers in pursuit of greater fluency and communicative confidence on the part of learners.

Furthermore, not all errors are of the same order and some have more serious consequences than others. For example, selecting the wrong vocabulary item or mispronouncing it may affect communication whereas a grammatical error may not. On the other hand, some grammatical errors may make it impossible to work out the intended meanings.

Research into language learning errors is active and continues to be fruitful. Increasingly, learners are encouraged to reflect on the nature of errors in and across languages rather than simply imitate and practise by repetition a set of carefully controlled forms. It is not likely, however, that error analyses can provide complete explanations of language learning processes. (see **contrastive hypothesis; fluency**)

ESL ESL is an abbreviation for English as a Second Language. English is learned as a second language in countries where English is institutionalized, that is, it is used as a medium of instruction in schools, as a language of business, law and government, and/or as a language of everyday communication. English is a second language in countries such as Singapore, Nigeria, India, the Philippines. (see **EFL**)

ESP This stands for English for Special (or Specific) Purposes. It refers to programmes in English teaching where the needs of the learners are precisely specified. ESP courses might include: English for Academic Purposes (**EAP**); English for Science and

Technology (EST); English for Banking. The term LSP (Language for Special Purposes) is also sometimes used.

EST   see (**ESP**)

exchange structure   (see **discourse analysis**)

false beginner   A term used to describe a language learner who is not literally beginning a course from the beginning. A false beginner already has some experience of learning the relevant language but lacks confidence and feels more comfortable following a course for beginners. Some language courses are specifically designed with false beginners in mind.

feedback   (see **discourse analysis**)

field, tenor and mode   Field, tenor and mode are major constituents of the functional theories of language developed by Michael Halliday. These concepts help to explain how language users interpret the social contexts or textual environments in which meanings are made. The 'field' of discourse refers to the 'subject matter' or topic of a stretch of language (e.g. the weather, geography, the local football team's failure). It refers to what is happening and to the nature of the social context in which meanings are made. The 'tenor' of discourse refers to the participants within a social exchange of meanings. The precise tenor of a particular stretch of language will be conditioned by the role relationships which obtain, particularly the status and relative power of the participants. This will condition the **formality** of the language used. The 'mode' of discourse refers to the expectations of the participants concerning the role played by language itself within a context or situation. Within the conceptual framework of mode, the channel or medium of communication (e.g. Is it spoken or some combination of the two?) will be especially significant. Also important is the rhetorical mode, that is, what is being achieved by the text, spoken or written, in terms of categories such as 'persuasive', 'didactic', 'expository' and so on. To summarize:

field – What is happening? What is the text about?
tenor – Who are taking part?
mode – What is the language itself doing?

fluency The term fluency normally describes language production which has features associated with native speakers. Second or foreign language learners who are fluent in that language speak and use the language naturally and with ease. They can communicate ideas and feelings effectively. They can produce language with use of pauses, intonation and interactive features close to a native speaker, though pronunciation will not necessarily be perfect. Fluency is often contrasted with accuracy. Accuracy refers to a learner's ability to produce grammatically correct language which can sometimes be to the exclusion of a fluent command of the language. It is widely accepted that the main goal of language teaching is to help learners use the target language accurately *and* fluently. (see also **communicative approach**)

foreigner talk Foreigner talk describes the ways in which people talk to others who are not native speakers of a language and who they perceive to be not wholly competent in that language. This process can take the form of speaking more loudly and slowly, extended repetition and simplified grammar. (see also **caretaker language**)

formality / informality These are terms in stylistic studies, essentially at either end of a continuum. Used to identify the linguistic features of any text, they range from those usually identified as appropriate to more impersonal social contexts (formal), to those appropriate to intimate and familiar social contexts (informal).

frames   (see **schema theory**)

frequency   It has always been a challenge for applied linguists and language teachers to specify the relative frequencies of words within a language. Recent projects such as the computer-based **COBUILD** project have made that challenge easier to meet and will continue to provide valuable information about the most frequent words in English, both spoken and written, their occurrence in different contexts of use and the patterns they form with other words. However, applications to teaching are not as straightforward as may sometimes appear. The most frequent words in a language are not necessarily the easiest to learn and they are often words with the widest range of different meanings. The most frequent words in a language may also not be the most useful to a learner in the earliest stages of language learning; less frequent words from a specific classroom or curriculum environment may be more immediately useful. Information about frequency of vocabulary and grammatical structures will, however, continue to be supplied in the future with even greater precision and language teachers cannot fail to benefit from it.

functional linguistics   (systemic–functional linguistics)   Functional linguistics has particular relevance for language teaching as well as other branches of applied linguistics such as **stylistics**. It is a particular theory of language which adopts a view of language as social interaction. Within functional linguistics, grammar is seen as a network of 'systems' of interrelated contrasts within which choices of one structure, in contrast with another, signal a particular meaning. Functional linguistics concentrates on the semantic and pragmatic aspects of meaning. There is a primary focus on language in use rather than on language as an abstract system and the models of analysis developed within functional linguistics are therefore of particular use for the analyses of naturally occurring spoken and written texts, often those produced within educational contexts.

gender The relationship between language and gender has been extensively studied during the last decade. The study of the ways in which gender is marked in different languages is important for purposes of language learning and contrastive study can form the basis for courses in **language awareness**. The main emphasis and interest has, however, been on the ways in which men and women are differently positioned, usually to the disadvantage of women, by particular uses of language. Studies range from the generic use of *man* (for women *and* men) or *he* (*A student should submit projects by Dec. 12th. Otherwise **he** will be penalized.*) to the ways in which texts such as advertisements or popular fiction reinforce stereotypes of female behaviour (for example, that women are passive, subservient to men and exist primarily as objects for men to view). Further sociolinguistic studies explore the ways in which women code-switch differently from men, with women moving more regularly towards standard language norms of grammar and pronunciation. Courses in language awareness and **KAL** (Knowledge About Language) normally include studies of language and gender as main components.

genre Theories of genre and precise accounts of the characteristic linguistic formations of different genres have evolved in order to help teachers and pupils understand some of the ways in which the following two texts (written by junior school children) **do** different things:

A long time ago there was a kangaroo who did not
have a tail and all the animals laughed at him and

31

that made him sad. How did he get it back? he got it back by dipping his tail into lolly-pop siarp [syrup]. The animals started to like him and then they played with him.

Would you like it? I would not because it would be most annoing.

The End

*   *   *

'Sharks'! When people think of sharks they think of harsh, savage fish that attack at sight as a matter of fact they are completly wrong. Although there has been reports of shark attacks these are very rare. Most sharks won't even come near the shore so people swimming near the shore can consider themselves almost guaranteed safe.

Sharks have special sense organs that can sense things up to 1 mile away. The shark uses fins to balance itself and it has to keep swimming or else it will sink. The shark's teeth are razor blade sharp and although you can only see two layers of teeth there are many in the jaw. Usually smaller fish follow the sharks around in hope of gathering up scraps that the shark may leave.

There are certain broad distinctions which apply to these texts. The first text could be said to be chronologically organized; whereas the latter is less concerned with a sequence of events through time and more concerned to convey a body of information. The former is chronological; the latter is non-chronological.

However, more precise description reveals differences in language which enable further distinction. The 'kangaroo' text, for example, locates events in the past tense, has connectives which order the text in an essentially temporal way and individuates main participants by the use of indefinite nouns (specific names would be equally appropriate in such a text). By contrast, the 'shark' text, which is an extract from a longer text, employs a simple present tense which serves to generalize actions; the text is organized not so much temporally as in terms of logical or explanatory relations which are signalled in the conjunctions (*because*, *in hope of*). The references to the shark are similarly not to an individual creature but to a general phenomenon of the mammal kingdom; hence the *shark* and *sharks* generalize and do not specify a singular individual entity. These linguistic differences enable us to distinguish the first text as belonging to a narrative genre and the latter as belonging to an information report genre.

Different genres are also differently staged. For example, a narrative genre may be divided into four main stages or schematic structures as follows:

1 orientation   Who are the participants? When did the action take place? Where?
2 complicating action   What happened then? What problems occurred?
3 resolution   How was the problem resolved?
4 coda   What moral can be drawn from the action?

In the 'kangaroo' text, it can be seen that the first sentence encapsulates both orientation and complicating action. The second, third and fourth sentences involve a resolution, and the final two sentences a (personalized) coda. A report genre is more simply constructed, with a stage in which the phenomenon is generally defined, and a stage in which information about the specific characteristics of the phenomenon is given. Thus, in the following report text by a six-year-old child, the first sentence has a structure of general classification:

The Bat
The bat is a nocturnal animal It lives in the dark

> there are long nosed bats and mouse eared bats also
> lettuce winged bats Bats hunt at nittg they sleep in the
> day and are very shy.

Genre theory has aroused controversy within the field of language in education. Advocates of genre-based approaches have argued for:

- more explicit classroom attention to grammatical forms and functions of language in writing different texts; accordingly, less reliance on intuitive, implicit or generalized language awareness
- the development of a wider range of genres of writing in schools; accordingly, less emphasis on the person-centred, narrative-based writing common in many English classes.

Opponents of genre theorists point to the dangers inherent in approaches which can be seen to rely on transmissive teaching methodologies; they doubt the claimed advantages of developing explicit generic knowledge among pupils (though they recognize its importance for teachers' own knowledge about language); and they question whether genres are quite as linguistically fixed as the above descriptions suggest. They point to the provenance of mixed genres and of the creative play with genres which involves changing and departing from norms.

The term genre is sometimes coexistent with the term **register**, especially in contexts of teaching English for special purposes (see **ESP**) where the emphasis is on the conventions specific to particular kinds of writing within the academic community.

A distinction between genre and register is useful as it enables a sharper focus on the functions of particular texts or types of text. Thus, a report is a superordinate term for a certain kind of text doing a particular job within a social context. Within the genre of report, there can thus be registers of weather report, school report, company report, and so on.

graded language / reading schemes Graded readers or reading scheme books are books which are specially written to enable the teaching of reading in a carefully graded and progressive way. In particular, the language used in such books is systematically selected so that children move from simple to more complex words and phrases. Such books also have the advantage that children get to know characters in familiar settings. They are of particular advantage in the teaching of second or foreign languages.

Graded or 'basal' readers are sometimes critized for being linguistically artificial and for inhibiting the use of real language. They can also lead to a lack of confidence in reading books which are outside the scheme. Many publishers have, however, recently developed highly imaginative and intelligently graded schemes which are written in ways which combine controlled language and natural usage. (see **real books**)

grammar In most traditions of linguistic description, grammar is seen as one of the three components of language structure – the other two are phonology and semantics. Grammar is also usually limited to the analysis of structures at and below sentence level. In recent years, however, with an increasing interest in **text** and **discourse**, the boundaries of the study of grammar have been extended. This area of study is usually called text grammar.

One ambiguity of the word comes from its popular use in a prescriptive sense ('bad grammar' as opposed to 'good grammar') to indicate features of language use that are regarded as 'mistakes'; for instance, dialect uses such as *I been* or *it were*. In this sense, the word is also used, unhelpfully, to refer to all manner of inaccuracies including spelling mistakes.

In modern linguistics, there are different approaches to the description of grammar. These differences are not wilful but arise from the different interests of linguists in developing their descriptions. Here are brief notes on the four main traditions.

1 descriptive grammar The purpose of descriptive grammar is to set out in a systematic and principled way the rules that appear to govern how a particular language is used. Thus, descriptive grammars deal with individual languages, e.g. English, Chinese or Finnish. They do not deal with universals of language. The rules identified are normally based on a corpus of data (a wide ranging sample of spoken and written language) and they are descriptive as opposed to **prescriptive**. Randolph Quirk *et al A Comprehensive Grammar of the English Language* is currently the most authoritative descriptive grammar of English.

2 systemic–functional grammar This tradition of grammar is associated with the work of Michael Halliday. Central to the analysis is the idea of choice. Each aspect of grammatical description is seen as a series of options from which the speaker or writer makes choices dependent on context and intention. Of particular importance in this type of analysis are the notions of transitivity, theme and **field / mode / tenor**. The specific value of this work is that grammar is related to meaning in a way that is not achieved in descriptive grammars, which tend to separate syntax and morphology, on the one hand, from semantics and **pragmatics**, on the other. (see also **functional linguistics**)

3 transformational–generative grammar (TG) The American linguist Noam Chomsky borrowed the term 'generative' from mathematics to describe this analysis of language. He was concerned to identify a set of rules and principles of creativity by which *all* instances of language production (surface structures) could be shown to be variations (transformations) of a small, finite set of basic or deep structures. Hence, transformational–generative grammar is more concerned with language universals than with the description of usage in a particular language.

4 pedagogical grammar The object of a pedagogical grammar is to

present the grammar of a language in ways which are pedagogically appropriate to learners (usually non-native learners) of a language. Pedagogical grammars do not necessarily follow any one theory, though they are likely to be descriptive in orientation. They are designed to provide information which is relevant for teaching and learning, for materials design, and for syllabus and curriculum development. Most modern course books or grammar teaching materials use game-like activities in which structures are learned and practised through the completion of meaningful and realistic tasks rather than by means of grammar drills.

grammar–translation method   This is a method of teaching foreign languages. It derives from traditional approaches to the teaching of Latin and Greek in the nineteenth century. It was also used to teach modern languages such as French and German and is still influential in the teaching of languages in many countries, particularly at university level. The approach is favoured because of the intellectual disciplines it imposes.

It is characterized by: a meticulous analysis of the target written language, especially its grammar; grammar taught deductively through the presentation and study of explicit rules; vocabulary learned from long bilingual word lists; and the paramount use of translation exercises.

The main goals of the grammar–translation method are to develop an ability to read prestigious literary texts, and to learn the disciplines of reading and writing the language accurately. The medium of instruction is the student's own native language. There is little or no systematic attention to the skills of speaking and listening.

grapho-phonic cue   (see **cues**)

holistic   Holistic or whole language approaches to language learning present language as a whole in real contexts of use not as a set of atomistic, decontextualized forms and structures. Holistic approaches stress the importance of language activities in which all four modes of reading, writing, listening and speaking are used, preferably in the context of group work in which language is learned through social interaction.

humanistic approaches (to language teaching) Humanistic approaches to language teaching adopt classroom strategies which are student-centred. They value the student's personal feelings, knowledge and experiences and encourage self-esteem and confidence in the student. Teaching techniques are designed to help students to be themselves and to share their ideas and feelings with others in the class. Humanistic approaches stress that by lowering the **affective filter** of learners (that is, their anxiety, their fear of making errors), a strong and lasting basis is created for developing linguistic knowledge. Language teaching approaches, which could be described as humanistic in orientation, include **Community Language Learning, suggestopedia**, the **Silent Way**.

IATEFL An abbreviation for International Association for Teachers of English as a Foreign Language.

information report genre   (see **genre**)

initiation   (see **discourse analysis**)

Input Hypothesis   The Input Hypothesis is a term widely used in connection with second language acquisition research. It states that for language acquisition to occur, it is necessary for a language learner to be exposed to language which is slightly beyond the learner's current understanding and competence. In this way, the learner learns to comprehend language by using clues based on the context in which the language is encountered. The term *1 + 1* is widely used in connection with this hypothesis;

1 + 1 means that, as a result of appropriately comprehensible input, the acquisition level of the learner moves from one stage to the next in a natural order of development. Parallels are often drawn with first language learning. Learners of a second language are said to require the kind of language input provided by **caretaker speech** in a first language, that is, language which contains sufficiently simplified and accessible codes to enable the next stage of language development to be reached.

interaction (classroom) Since the 1980s, there has been an increasing number of studies of classroom interaction. These have been facilitated by improvements in audio technology but have been motivated by an interest on the part of researchers in the kinds of classroom processes which support effective learning. The main focus is on interaction between teacher and pupil but also on the nature of pupils' collaborative learning in pairs and in groups. Most researchers undertake detailed analysis of the particular uses of language which characterize different styles of learning. Among the areas investigated are: questioning styles; the extent and character of teacher talk compared with pupil talk; gender differences in talk processes; the nature of exploratory talk. (see **collaborative learning**; **discourse analysis**)

interlanguage The term interlanguage refers to a transitional stage in learning a second or foreign language. As learners acquire a language, they acquire more and more knowledge about the target language, adding incrementally to an existing store. In the process of acquisition, they pass, however, through different stages in which accurate knowledge of the target language is mixed in ever changing proportions with hypotheses about the target language (which are being constantly revised), knowledge based on analogies with the mother-tongue and errors which result from the need simply to make oneself understood. In these transitional stages, control of the target language is partial. Learners possess a knowledge which is equivalent neither to L1 nor L2. This linguistic knowledge is their 'interlanguage'.

intertextuality   This is a recent term much used in text linguistics to explore literary language. It is essentially defined as 'texts in relation to other texts', i.e. in any given text (written or read), a continual 'dialogue' is being set up with other texts (both literary and non-literary) that exist outside it, both currently and historically. For example, Allan Ahlberg's *The Jolly Postman* plays on our awareness of famous fairy tales; and when e e cummings writes *all in green went my love riding*, he evokes the medieval ballad form.

intonation   Intonation is a term used in linguistic description to refer to an aspect of phonological study called suprasegmental phonology (see **phonology**). It refers to a study of those aspects of the sound system which operate *across* phonemic segments, i.e. patterns of pitch. This is the 'melody' or 'tone' of any utterance, usually identified on a continuum from 'high' to 'low'. Interest generally (but not exclusively) focuses on the final element of the tone movement in any one utterance, e.g.

What's the *time*?   Question   (rise)
It's twelve *o'clock*.   Statement   (fall)

Tone is therefore monitored in terms of the degree of rise and fall in relation to the high/low scale.

Frequently, intonation patterns convey attitudes of meaning, for example, degrees of emotional involvement (the higher the rise or fall of the voice, the greater the degree of involvement):

What a long symphony.   (high fall – indicates that it is boring)
What a magnificent symphony! (low fall – indicates that it is!)

Similarly, because a high rise indicates uncertainty, this pattern frequently occurs in questions:

Are you certain that it's true?   (high rise)

In general terms, the tone falls at the end of an utterance if it is a statement or an assertion. In studying language varieties (e.g. dialects, registers, styles of speech, etc.), it is particularly interesting to note how intonation patterns vary according to situation:

- the variations in intonation patterns associated with dialects (e.g. Yorkshire, Cornwall, etc.) and other 'Englishes' (e.g. Irish, Welsh, Australian, American)
- variations in the registers of English (e.g. football results, thought-for-the-day, the weather forecast)
- intonational variation in different styles of speech (e.g. casual conversation, formal lecture)
- the congruence (or otherwise) between the grammatical form of an utterance and the speech function expressed by intonation. For example, *She went yesterday* has the grammatical form of a statement, Subject–Verb–Adverb, but intonation can reflect either a statement or a question
- the differences of 'converting' the information flow of spoken language into written language forms, in particular, the relationship between punctuation and intonation.

An important function of intonation is that it signals grammatical structure. In this respect, it takes on the role in speech similar to that assigned to **punctuation** in writing. Yet, the spoken situation is capable of producing many more contrasts. Consider, for example, how the following sentence has to be rewritten to convey the contrasts of meaning that are produced by tone in speech:

John loves Mary   (as opposed to *Peter* loving Mary)
John *loves* Mary   (as opposed to *hating* her)
John loves *Mary*   (as opposed to *Julie*)

Traditionally, intonation has concentrated on utterance patterns and the links between them; and such patterns can be a useful focus for teachers in identifying speech–writing differences and the difficulties that pupils might have in coming to terms with the English writing system, i.e. writing is more than 'speech written down'. Developments in **communicative approaches** to language teaching have seen increasing emphasis on the teaching of intonation.

intonation and punctuation   There are some points to be made about the relationship between intonation and punctuation in writing. Many textbooks see punctuation simply as teaching learners to punctuate correctly (e.g. 'A sentence has a capital letter at the beginning and a full stop at the end.'). Writing is simply seen as speech with certain mechanics and conventions tagged on.

Units of meaning are primarily developed in speech by means of intonation and, to some extent, punctuation in writing reflects this (e.g. commas are sometimes used to indicate a change of intonation where, for example, one information unit finishes and another starts: *When I've finished washing up, I shall do the ironing*).

However, not all punctuation choices stem from intonational cues. For example, the choice of a semi-colon is usually a grammatical or textual choice. And larger units (such as paragraphs) only exist in writing; their essential characteristics have to be learned. There are thus two basic principles to choose from: punctuation according to grammar, and punctuation according to phonology. When clauses match up with tone groups, as in the above example, there are no problems. But, where they differ, writers move between the two according to their expressive purpose. The following sentences show different possibilities: **1** is mainly grammatical punctuation; **2** is mainly phonological punctuation.

1 For David, the decision came too late and, as the guard approached, he put his hands in the air.

2 For David the decision came too late, and as the guard approached he put his hands in the air.

As applied linguistics focuses increasingly on distinctions and differences between speech and writing, so will there be an increasing number of descriptions and insights relevant to the study and teaching of punctuation.

KAL KAL is a term now much used in discussions of the teaching of English as a Mother Tongue. It stands for Knowledge About Language. In accordance with the National Curriculum for English in England and Wales, pupils are introduced to a systematic study of the structure and functions of the English language. This commences formally at the secondary school stage and the study is normally undertaken in the context of pupils' own experiences of reading, writing and talk. The emphasis is on new exploratory and investigative approaches to language rather than on the decontextualized teaching of parts of speech which was associated with language study in the 1950s. Among the 'topics' for developing knowledge about language in the British National Curriculum are: differences between spoken and written English; literary language; language change; accents, dialects and standard Englishes; registers and varieties of English.

language acquisition   (see **learning (of language)**)

language across the curriculum   This is an approach to language teaching which emphasizes the teaching of language in relation to use across a whole school curriculum and which concentrates on the language requirements of particular school subjects.

language awareness   A term used in modern foreign language teaching and to a lesser extent in EFL/ESL teaching to refer to teaching which, during the process of language learning, draws

43

attention to aspects of the nature and functions of language. Proponents of greater language awareness argue that more explicit and conscious attention to the systematic organization of language is a prerequisite for success in language learning. (see **KAL**; **learning how to learn**)

language planning   Language planning is a field in which insights from linguistics, and in particular sociolinguistics, may be applied with relevance for the development of the policies of a national government. In particular, language planning involves the development and implementation of official policies concerning the place, function and status of different varieties of a language or of different languages within a country or community. Language planning is normally undertaken in relation to education and involves crucial decisions over the language which will form the medium of instruction in schools. Such decisions have inevitable implications both for national identity and for which languages will be maintained within a country.

However, language planning can also be less fundamental in nature. For example, language planning decisions involve: spelling reform; gender-free language policies; modernization of religious language; the removal of bureaucratic jargon.

Language planning decisions can invoke strong feelings of support and opposition and in some contexts such attitudes are not changed by official policies. The role of applied linguistics in exercises of language planning is to try to provide and evaluate evidence which relates to the social, cultural and educational consequences of planning decisions, although specific programmes with a linguistic basis, such as spelling reform, may be the direct result of linguistic theory and analysis. Most of those who formulate political decisions concerning language planning are unlikely to possess any specialized linguistic knowledge.

language use   (see **metalanguage**)

LARSP An abbreviation for Language Assessment, Remediation and Screening Procedure. LARSP is a detailed profile of grammatical development used for monitoring the progress of children with language handicaps.

learner-centred Learner-centred approaches to language teaching and to the language curriculum are aimed at those strategies and procedures which maximize language learning. Central to these approaches is a continuing consideration of the preferred learning processes and concerns of the learner. The main goal is to shape language learning as far as possible in accordance with the needs of individual learners. Such a goal places less focus on the teacher's judgement of those needs.

A learner-centred approach does not, however, make the teacher invisible. On the contrary, the teacher often has to be more active, to be better prepared and to work harder than in more teacher-centred approaches. The crucial task for the teacher is to create conditions in which learners can collaborate with each other, ask their own questions about the target language, evaluate their own language learning goals, better understand their own preferred styles of teaching and learning. Many of the techniques developed as part of **communicative approaches** to language teaching methodology lend themselves to a learner-centred approach. (see **collaborative learning**; **learning how to learn**)

learner typology Learner typologies are an important aspect of studies in language acquisition for the capacities for learning another language depend on a range of factors including age, motivation and previous foreign language learning experience. Furthermore, learners learn in different ways and have different preferences. For example, some prefer to learn through listening and oral practice; others prefer to learn by seeing the language written down first. Some prefer to learn words in lists with translation equivalents; others prefer to learn words by rote repetition. Different learners also prefer some teaching styles to others with some learners feeling comfortable in small group work, others feeling more comfortable with a more teacher-led presentation. Teachers are becoming increasingly aware of the need to recognize and plan for different types of learner and to encourage learners to recognize their own best learning practices. (see **learning how to learn**)

learning (of language) In some theories, language learning is opposed to language acquisition. Learning results from explicit teaching about the rules and structures of the target language. Learners learn such facts about the language consciously and draw on this knowledge as a **monitor** or corrective mechanism when producing the target language. Language learning normally depends on formal teaching, correction of students' errors and on a student's ability to utilize the learned rules of the language, sometimes by explicitly verbalizing the rules. Although 'acquisition' and 'learning' are seen as two distinctive ways of developing competence, most research points to the need for teaching strategies which synthesize rather than oppose (see **acquisition of language**)

learning how to learn This describes strategies used in the classroom which help language learners to reflect on their own learning preferences and on the styles of teaching which are most effective for them in learning a language. The aim is to make learners a little more self-conscious about their own learning successes in reading, writing, speaking and listening. Many teachers believe that such procedures lead to more effective learning.

level Level is a term used by linguists, usually in the context of levels of analysis, and illustrates how any stretch of language (spoken or written) may be analysed from different perspectives (i.e. on different levels). Therefore, any text may be viewed on any of the following levels:

- discourse (whole text)
- grammar / syntax (e.g. sentence, clause, phrase)
- vocabulary
- morphology
- phonology / graphology

Frequently, linguists talk about 'top–down' or '**bottom–up**' approaches to language study. A bottom–up approach to language description would look first at the lower levels (e.g. graphology and morphology); whereas a top–down approach considers a text at discourse level initially and then relates this analysis to specific features at lower levels. (see **bottom–up (processing)**)

lexicography Lexicography refers to the process of compiling dictionaries. The past twenty years have seen significant advances in foreign language lexicography. (see **COBUILD; dictionary**)

lingua franca A lingua franca is a language which is used as a principal means of communication between groups of people who have different mother-tongues. Another term for lingua franca is auxiliary language. In a country such as Nigeria, the lingua franca is English; in Mozambique, the lingua franca is Portuguese; in India, the lingua franca is either Hindi or English, depending on the social context.

literature (in language teaching) The 1980s saw an increase in the use of literary texts in the language classroom after a long period in which such texts were not felt to serve the utilitarian goals associated with a language course. It is now accepted that responding to more creative and non-utilitarian uses of language is an important part of language competence. Carefully selected literary texts can also be motivating and enjoyable to read and can assist learners to understand the cultural contexts, both contemporary and historical, in which the literature is set. Methodologies for the teaching of literature have drawn on standard language teaching strategies for teaching texts and have tended to focus learners' attention on the ways in which language is used. Such methods are also widely known as language-based approaches to literature.

Stylistic analysis has played a significant part in the teaching of literature, especially at more advanced levels in the study of second or foreign language literatures. Advocates of the teaching of stylistics argue that systematic attention to language use and to a writer's stylistic choices has two main benefits. First, a sound basis is provided for explaining how specific literary effects work and literary meanings are constructed. The greater awareness of language structures possessed by learners of a language can be an advantage here. Second, by systematic reference to language use, students of literature can acquire both greater skill and confidence in the interpretation of literary texts.

The basic starting point for much work in the field of literature in language teaching is that literature is made from language. Closer integration between literary and language studies is therefore of mutual benefit. Stylistics is sometimes also referred to as literary linguistics.

Recent work on the literature curriculum has stressed the advantages of studying not simply the canonical texts of the culture of native speakers of the target language. Instead, literatures in English are increasingly incorporated into literature programmes. These are second language literatures written in English and produced in countries such as Kenya, Nigeria, India or the Philippines where strong literary traditions exist. (see also **EIL**; **stylistics**)

Look and Say Look and Say is a term used to describe an approach to the teaching of reading. It is also sometimes called the 'whole word' method. As the terms suggest, the approach is based on the principle that children learn to read by seeing whole words many times. The main aim is to help children to process longer and more meaningful stretches of language than is normally allowed in 'phonic' approaches which break words down into constituent sounds and letters. By this method, children come to know the shapes of words and even phrases. Look and Say methods are necessary in the case of the many words which do not have regular sound–letter relationships. The approach has been criticized for its lack of clear principles of grading. (see **phonics**)

LSP   (see **ESP**)

metadiscourse   Texts both written and spoken are composed of two different types of information. The principal type is the message, that is, what the text is about. The second type is information which guides the reader/listener in two different ways: either it indicates the structure of the text or explains the nature of the text itself, or it makes provision for the reader/listener to recognize the writer/speaker's point of view. For example,

1 *In the first section of chapter one we will discuss the nature of spoken discourse.*
2 *The following example will clarify this point.*
3 *I believe that . . .*
4 *It certainly seems true that . . .*

This textual guidance is termed metadiscourse. It is important that such guidance is used appropriately. Too much and the message will be lost; too little and it will be difficult for the reader/listener to process the principal information. The frequency and type of metadiscourse used in a text is variable and depends on a number of different factors: novice readers, whether mother-tongue or second language learners, require more support in the text and as a consequence tolerate more metadiscourse than mature readers. Some genres require more metadiscourse than others: an argument, for example, which has a more complex structure than a narrative, demands that writers/speakers support their readers/listeners' understanding by employing metadiscourse in their text.

The most common tendency is for students to use too little metadiscourse because they assume too much prior knowledge on the part of their reader/examiner/teacher. Thus, being made aware of metadiscourse means that students can become more sensitive to the needs of their audience and, as a consequence, they can start to judge the proportion and type of metadiscourse which is required in the production of a successful text.

metalanguage Technically, metalanguage is a higher-level language used to talk about an area of study (as in the 'language of mathematics' or the 'language of nuclear physics'). In applied linguistics, it refers generally to language used to discuss language use. Aspects of metalanguage inform much day-to-day discussion of how language is and can be used. Most of the terms in this A–Z are metalingual.

methodology Methodology refers to the range of teaching methods, procedures and strategies adopted by a teacher in order to help learners to acquire a language. Methodologies do not have to be influenced by applied linguistics but they are likely to be sounder and more successful if they draw on insights into processes of language development provided by applied linguistic research. It is also likely that the more teachers understand about the structure and organization of language, the more principled and systematic can be their choices and design of language learning activities.

miscue / miscue analysis (see **cues**)

Monitor Model The Monitor Model or Monitor Hypothesis is a significant aspect of the natural approach to language learning. It is central to the distinction drawn between language acquisition and language learning. It is connected with the approaches and methods of language teaching associated with the American applied linguist Stephen Krashen.

The 'Monitor' is a conscious process of editing or monitoring the language we produce in the course of learning a language. It is seen by Krashen as opposed to the natural and subconscious processes of acquisition of language and works against such processes when the learner checks and corrects language output. The Monitor Hypothesis thus claims that the Monitor is explicit, learned knowledge of the rules of the language. Learners operate the Monitor in order to try to ensure that the language they produce is accurate and correct.

For Krashen and his associates, conscious learning of a language cannot lead to successful acquisition. For them, the Monitor inhibits fluent communication by focusing on the forms and rules of the language. Learners who worry too much about making mistakes are overusing the Monitor and allowing it to get in the way of their natural processes of language acquisition.

mother-tongue Mother-tongue is a term which is sometimes used loosely as synonymous with community language. However, there are several difficulties with the term:

1 For many pupils the language of their community may not be their 'mother-tongue' or their first language.
2 The 'mother-tongue' may be one dialect of a language that has several variations (e.g. Italian or Punjabi).
3 The term is ambiguous because it carries connotations of being the mother's language but could also be interpreted as

the language of the mother country – ambiguous, for instance, in the case of a language such as Yiddish.

4 There are dangers inherent in seeing mother-tongue or 'native' speakers as superior users of the language or as seeing mother-tongue speakers of English as better qualified to teach the language. Non-native speakers with a different mother-tongue may know, use and teach the language more effectively.

5 A mother-tongue speaker of English may know only one dialect of English. (see also **dialect**; **Standard English**)

multilingualism   Multilingualism refers to the knowledge by an individual or a community of three or more languages. Multilingualism is common in many parts of the world, although one language will normally act as a lingua franca or main vehicle of communication between the speakers or as a standard language for written communication for use in the media and / or as a medium of instruction in schools. In some countries, the existence of multilingualism or of multilingual communities is seen as a problem; in other countries, it is seen as a resource which can be mobilized for national advantage and as a positive aspect of nationhood.

narrative genre   (see **genre**)

NATE   An abbreviation for National Association for the Teaching of English. NATE is the main professional organization in the United Kingdom for teachers who are principally concerned with the teaching of English as a Mother-Tongue. Parallel organizations in the United States and Australia are National Council of Teachers of English and Australian Association for the Teaching of English.

Natural Approach   The Natural Approach is a general term for an approach to language teaching. It has been most extensively developed in the United States. It has affinities with the **commun-**

icative approach and is **humanistic** in orientation. Central to the theory are hypotheses about learning procedures and conditions for learning. These are explained under other entries, e.g. **affective filter; Input Hypothesis; learning (of language); Monitor Model; Natural Order Hypothesis**. One criticism of the natural approach is that its advocates may underestimate the difficulties of reproducing in the second language classroom conditions for learning which parallel the conditions under which a first language is learned.

Natural Order Hypothesis According to the Natural Order Hypothesis the acquisition of the structures of a language takes place in a predictable order. The hypothesis arose as a result of studies of learners of a number of different languages which drew attention to the fact that the foreign language learners appear to make similar errors regardless of the language they are learning and regardless of their language background. The conclusion was drawn that universal procedures of language development were at work and that learners were following a natural 'internal' syllabus which the 'external' syllabus of the classroom may need to take fuller account of. The hypothesis also claims to show that there are clear similarities between the natural order of a first language and the order in which a second or foreign language is learned.

However, studies undertaken so far are limited; only a very small number of structures (mainly grammatical morphemes such as plural 's', past tense -*ed* and -*ing* forms) have been examined and not much attention has been given to languages other than English. It is clearly helpful to know that under normal circumstances learners naturally learn the progressive – *ing* form of the verb before the third person 's' and that the active is more easily taught before the passive. But claims for universal order need to be treated with caution until longitudinal studies have been undertaken in a wider range of languages.

naturalness Several applied linguists have argued that the concept of naturalness is important to processes of language learning. To produce natural English is to produce English which a fluent native-speaker of English would produce. It is pointed out that the sentences found in grammars of English and in course books are not always examples of natural English. They are often made up by the teacher in order to illustrate a point about English structure or usage. Such language can sound contrived and large databases of English such as the **COBUILD** corpus can demonstrate that such instances are not found in naturally occurring text. It is thus argued that only natural English should serve as pedagogic examples. Other applied linguists argue that language has to be contrived for purposes of language learning so that the learner can easily access the relevant rules. Simplified language can be justified on these grounds. Others also argue that the authenticity or naturalness of the context in which language is used is more important than absolute authenticity of language use.

non-chronological text (see **genre**)

notional–functional syllabus This is a syllabus for teaching a foreign language which stresses the kinds of meanings learners need to express themselves and the kinds of language function needed to produce such meanings. Examples of notions include meanings and concepts such as time, quantity, location, frequency, motion, etc. Examples of functions include such communicative acts as requesting, describing, expressing likes and dislikes, and using language to mark social relationships. Notional–functional approaches have had a formative influence on the **communicative approach** to language teaching.

oral A term used to distinguish the form of the language used as distinctively *spoken* as opposed to written. For example, an oral test or an oral examination. (see **spoken and written language**)

orientation   (see **genre**)

overgeneralizing   This term is used to identify a particular aspect of a child's initial learning of a language. For example, when experimenting with a particular grammatical feature of the language (e.g. the past tense form of the verb), a child might extend the past tense rule to contexts not found in adult language. Hence, you often find children saying *wented* and *goed* rather than *went*, thereby overgeneralizing in not yet taking account of irregular forms.

paralinguistics   The study of non-verbal phenomena such as gesture, body language and facial expressions which reinforce what is said.

pedagogical grammar   (see **grammar**)

phatic   Phatic communion is the use of language (e.g. *Nice day today?*) mainly for a social function or for social contact.

phonics   Phonics is a term used to describe approaches to the teaching of reading based on sound–letter combinations. Thus the word *cat* is taught as the relationship between the letters C-A-T and the sounds which those letters represent. Phonic approaches give a rationale for 'sounding out' new words but there are two main objections to any teaching of reading which is based exclusively on phonics. First, careful phonetic grading results in words and phrases which are at best artificial and which often bear no relation to real language. Second, hundreds of English words do not conform to phonic rules. Most teachers agree that some phonic clues help children to decode words when they are learning how to read.

phonology   This is a linguistic term which, like its synonym, phonemics, refers specially to the study and description of language as a sound system. In this respect, it differs significantly from phonetics, a term used to describe how sounds are articulated and produced. Phonology is the study of those patterns and contrasts of sound specific to any one language selected from the much wider range of sounds that a human voice can actually produce. In any one language, then, a limited number of distinctive sounds (phonemes) combine to form words.

It is the particular aim of phonology, therefore, to show how sounds are patterned, i.e. sounds analysed in discrete segments. (NB This particular area of description is referred to as segmental phonology; the study of sounds which extend across segments is referred to as supra-segmental phonology (see **intonation**).) For example, the replacement or substitution of single phonemes can produce words with different meanings: *pig* becomes *big*; *tin* becomes *din*, *Kate* becomes *gate*.

From an applied linguistic perspective, the study of such sound patterns might well be useful in the following areas:

- the range of accent features in both regional dialects and national and international languages
- the ways in which sound patterns can help/hinder reading development
- how sound/symbol correspondence (or lack of it) relates to the development and teaching of approaches to spelling
- how patterns relate to the organization of meaning in literature, specifically in the language of poetry.

pidgin   (see **creoles**)

pitch   (see **intonation**)

pragmatics   Pragmatics is the study of the semantics of utterances with an emphasis on the meanings created by speakers and listeners in interpersonal contexts. Students of pragmatics are interested in the contextual functions of language, the intentions and presuppositions of speakers and the effects produced on listeners. Pragmatists do not ask 'What does X mean?' but 'What do you mean by X?' The study tends to confine itself to single exchanges or relatively short utterances; this distinguishes it from discourse analysis which is a study of the linguistic patterns occurring across longer stretches of text.

For example, the meaning of the utterance *She's not that enthusiastic* will depend upon the context of the situation:

Context A

Speaker: parent   Hearer: neighbour
Place: kitchen   Time: mid-morning
Situation: The neighbour is inquiring about the parent's daughter and her interest in hiking. The neighbour offers to take her on a weekend tour of the Lake District. The parent replies, *'She's not that enthusiastic!'*

Context B

Speaker: teacher   Hearer: parent
Place: school   Time: late afternoon
Situation: The parent has come to see the teacher about her daughter's progress at school and asks about her interests in pursuing languages at A level. The teacher replies, *'She's not that enthusiastic.'*

prescriptive Prescriptive views of language state that one variety of a language is inherently superior to other varieties of that language. Accordingly, that one superior variety should be codified and taught as the correct or standard version. Prescriptivism is especially prevalent in grammar and pronunciation where certain absolute rules of correctness are laid down and where deviations from such rules are denounced as mistakes or as incorrect usage.

A descriptive view of language is less concerned with what ought to be said or written, nor with what absolutely correct standards of usage are. Instead, descriptivism is concerned with the facts of language use and with describing the way a language is actually used. Descriptivists do not prescribe; they are not preoccupied with right or wrong grammar or pronunciation; they do not attempt to evaluate usage nor to oppose natural processes of language change over time.

Most approaches adopted by contemporary linguists are descriptive in orientation.

process and product   These terms are mainly employed in relation to the teaching of writing; however, there is in most areas of the language curriculum a tension between views of language as process and language as product. In general, a product-oriented approach focuses on the end result of the learning process – what it is that learners are expected to be able to know and do. A process-oriented approach focuses on the kinds of methodologies which promote various aspects of language competence. Thus, product-based approaches to the teaching of writing will stress the importance of learners imitating correct models and of the use of correct sentence-based grammar; process-based approaches stress the importance of learners working through several drafts and discussing changes to their text in the course of producing a final version. However, absolute distinctions between process and product are untenable and most language classes involve an integration of process- and product-oriented procedures. (see **bottom–up (processing)**)

process syllabus   A process syllabus is not a list of objectives nor the kind of organization of language content associated with a course book. Instead, a process syllabus specifies questions and decisions concerning content, methods, and preferred learning styles which need to be addressed during a course. These are questions and decisions which have to be *jointly* resolved by teacher and learners in the *process* of their week-by-week classroom meetings. Second, a process syllabus specifies a bank of alternative procedures from which teacher and learners select after they have evaluated their joint progress at each stage of the language course. A process syllabus is a means by which teacher and taught plan and follow their own classroom syllabus.

product   (see **process and product**)

productive / receptive   (see **active / passive knowledge of language**)

projects   Language projects involve learners in studying the language in an exploratory and investigative manner. Areas for investigation can range from an interlingual comparison of particular language forms to more open-ended examination of particular accents and dialects to topics such as the language of newspapers or advertising. Projects are seen as basic to the development of a comprehensive **language awareness** or Knowledge About Language (**KAL**). They encourage learner autonomy and independence.

pronunciation   Pronunciation refers to the way in which sounds are produced. Many learners find it difficult to achieve native-speaker-like pronunciation, particularly when sounds and combinations of sound in the target language do not occur in the learner's own language. Some teachers and applied linguists do, however, question whether it is desirable to pronounce like a native-speaker. They prefer to encourage learners to develop their own distinctive pronunciation, preferably associated with their country of origin, as long as clear communication is not affected. (see **EIL**; **Standard English**)

punctuation   (see **intonation and punctuation**)

real books 'Real books' is a term which describes a particular kind of book but which has also come to be used to describe an approach to the teaching of reading. 'Real books' or 'whole books' mean that teachers teach reading using the kind of books which might be bought in a bookshop. Advocates of real books oppose graded readers or books in reading schemes on the grounds that controlled or graded language is artificial and cannot create meaningful experiences for the reader. Real books are believed to be more motivating to read. It is sometimes alleged that the 'real books' approach means that children are not taught to read but are simply exposed to the books so that they learn to read in the same way that they pick up the spoken language. There is little truth in these allegations. Most teachers use a mix of different methods for the teaching of reading; most schools teach children to read using a combination of real books and books from reading schemes. (see **graded language**)

Received Pronunciation (RP)   (see **accent**)

reference   (see **cohesion**)

register   This is a rather imprecise term which describes the kind of language use appropriate to a particular function in a situational context: for example, a legal register or a register of advertisements. Features of language are selected in accordance with context, purpose, and the relation of the language user to an audience. The term register is often used as a synonym for language varieties. (see **genre**)

resolution   (see **genre**)

response   (see **discourse analysis**)

restricted code   (see **code**)

role-play Language learners role-play when they take on a part and act out, almost as if they were in a play, specific actions associated with the part. Advocates of role-play in language teaching stress the high degrees of authenticity which role-play can produce. Some teachers believe that really authentic tasks have to involve learners in roles which they can believe in and involve actions which are genuinely close to the kinds of situations in which learners are likely to find themselves.

Sapir–Whorf hypothesis The Sapir–Whorf hypothesis was developed by two American linguist–anthropologists, Edward Sapir and Benjamin Lee Whorf in the earlier part of this century. The hypothesis states that the structure of a language determines the way in which we think and that different languages will therefore encode the world differently. Thus, concepts found in the language of one people may not be available to speakers of other languages. An example would be the fact that Australian aboriginal languages have few words for numerals. According to the hypothesis, it is said that Aborigines lack the concept of number and experience difficulties in counting properly.

The hypothesis has not been validated. Certainly, conceptual distinction and recall are easier if appropriate words are available but there is no evidence to suggest that conceptual differences between cultures restrict one group of people or advantage another. Aborigines who learn English as a second language have not experienced marked difficulties with the language of the number system in English.

Sapir and Whorf's work has, however, been influential on studies of the relationship between language and culture.

scenarios   (see **schema theory**)

schema theory Schema theory studies the relationship between background knowledge, language and comprehension. Research is rooted in cognitive psychology and a wide variety of terms **are** used. In addition to schema (plural schemata), terms such as frames, scripts and scenarios are used. The basic theory states that human memory stores sets of stereotypical situations or experiences which enable us to interpret new situations. Such schemata also enable us to make predictions about what we might expect to experience in a given context. Applied linguists have also studied how interpretive procedures are used to match schematic knowledge and the knowledge of the forms of language. Other versions of the theory also explain how we can understand texts such as the following much-quoted example:

A: *There's the phone.*
B: *I'm in the bath.*
A: *OK.*

Here, schematic knowledge of the functions of these linguistically unconnected phrases enables us to interpret the stretch of language as coherent. For example, the first utterance can be interpreted as a request to answer the phone. The second utterance can be interpreted as an explanation of an inability to comply. The third utterance can be interpreted as an acceptance of the excuse. Research into schema has been especially useful in its application to the design of tasks and exercises for teaching, listening and reading comprehension. (see also **bottom–up (processing)**)

scripts   (see **schema theory**)

self-access   Self-access refers to a process whereby learners are taught to be increasingly autonomous as learners. They are guided to materials by means of which they plot their own paths for learning a language, selecting tasks, exercises or projects which will enable them to practise aspects of the language which they decide are in need of further development or reinforcement. The process should be carefully and regularly monitored by teachers and, where feasible, closely integrated into the target syllabus. Many language schools and centres now have self-access centres where all materials are stored and where students can go to work independently.

semantic cue   (see **cues**)

Silent Way   The Silent Way is the name given to a method of language teaching developed by Caleb Gattegno. It makes use of mime, gesture, all kinds of visual aids, including colour-coded, pronunciation wall charts and, in particular, Cuisiniere rods. These are a set of rods of different lengths and colours which are used by the teacher to encourage students to talk. Particularly in the early stages, the learners talk intensively about the rods using a simple, controlled vocabulary and some basic verbs (e.g. *This is a green rod*). Learners then build up more complex structures (e.g. *Take the long red rod and give it to Claire*). During this process the teacher remains relatively silent (hence 'the silent way'), the aim being to encourage the student of the language to be increasingly self-reliant and independent of the teacher. The teacher guides the whole process but by saying as little as possible. Learners have to learn how to test for themselves their hypotheses about how the target language works. It is principally by such means, Gattegno and his followers argue, that learners properly retain grammatical structures and vocabulary items at a deeper level of awareness.

The learning theories which underly Gattegno's work are that learning a language is more effective if learners take responsibility for their learning by discovering meanings for themselves rather than simply repeating input from the teacher, and if learning is through a process of problem solving rather than through a process of memorization. The Silent Way aims to put into practice a method of **learning how to learn**.

spelling The teaching of spelling remains controversial. There are strong views in favour of spelling being 'caught' rather than taught; that is, exposure to the orthographic system of a language, usually through reading, is felt to be a sufficient basis for learning to spell. The belief that spelling has to be systematically taught recognizes that insights from the field of linguistics can be valuably applied to this process. Linguistics has been demonstrated to be of particular relevance to the teaching of spelling in the following main areas: sound–symbol correspondences; morpho-phonemic relations (the connection between individual sounds, morphemes and letter sequences); and historical semantics (the recognition of how some spelling rules are dictated by the historical origins or derivations of words).

spoken and written language Spoken and written are two major modes of language organization. In their extreme forms, for example, a casual conversation between friends and a formal business letter, there are a number of significant linguistic differences. However, spoken and written language are best seen as sets of tendencies. For example, written language tends to be characterized by nouns formed from verbs whereas spoken language tends to contain more verbal processes. Thus:

1 The *completion* of the job will take seven days.
2 We will *complete* the job in seven days.

Sentence **1** tends to be written and sentence **2** tends to be spoken. There are, however, many other categories which distinguish spoken and written language tendencies and there are, of course, many examples, such as much contemporary advertising copy, of one category overlapping into another. (see **formality / informality**)

Standard English   Standard English has been defined as:

> that variety of English which is usually used in print
> and which is normally taught in schools and to non-
> native speakers using the language. It is also the variety
> which is normally spoken by educated people and used
> in news broadcasts and other similar situations.

There is a particular relationship between Standard English
and written forms not just in Great Britain but internationally.
Its grammar and vocabulary have been codified. It is used extensively in education, including formal, public written exam-
inations in all subjects. Beyond school, it is used widely in public
and professional life. In this respect, many mother-tongue curriculum documents stress the entitlement of pupils to Standard
English: not to give access to Standard English would be to
disempower pupils socially and culturally. Other countries
also have a Standard English. For example, there is Standard
American English and Standard Australian English.

Standard English and spoken language

For some pupils, Standard English is a native dialect, that is,
they are brought up speaking it. This group is not restricted
geographically, and speakers of Standard English do not necessarily reveal their geographical origins in the grammar or vocabulary of their speech. Some speakers of Standard English speak it
with the accent termed **Received Pronunciation (RP)** or with an
accent approximating to it. This accent has its origins in the
variety of English spoken in public schools and within the pro-
fessions and the media. It is the basis on which English pronunciation is often taught internationally. Standard English can,
however, be spoken with any accent.

It is important to stress that in Great Britain today nearly all
dialects are readily understood if they are spoken clearly. Standard English will be one of the most familiar due to its intensive
media use.

Standard English and appropriacy

Though it has been extensively described and codified, Standard English is not an homogeneous entity; it is subject to historical change and variation across the world. Standard English has many sub-varieties. For example, Standard Scientific English, Standard Medical English and Standard Business English are all different from each other and there are different varieties of Business English, some formal and legalistic, some technical, some persuasive, which are used on different occasions and for different purposes. There are contexts in which Standard Spoken English is appropriate and desirable (for example, in most formal interview situations, or in public discourse with larger, unknown audiences); but there are other situations in which formal Standard English may be out of place (such as small group discussions with colleagues or friends), and in which more informal, local dialect forms may be more appropriate – as long as communication is clear and comprehensible. (see **accent**; **dialect**; **EIL**)

standard language   (see **creoles**)

stylistics   Stylistics is the application of linguistics to the study of linguistic variation. It is particularly concerned with an analysis of the choices writers make. Linguistic approaches to the study of literary style stress the importance of particular stylistic choices for an interpretation of the meanings of a complete poem, or drama or novel or short story. Some stylistic studies have also attempted to characterize the style of individual authors. Stylistic analysis is an important component in courses in literature (in language teaching), especially at an advanced level, where an aim is to provide students with a systematic basis on which to build interpretations as well as an appreciation of the way language can be developed to its fullest creative limits. (see **literature (in language teaching)**)

substitution   (see **cohesion**)

suggestopedia   Suggestopedia is an approach to language learning based on suggestology, the science of suggestion. It is associated with the work of a Bulgarian psychiatrist–educator, Georgie Lozanov. The approach is based on the view that the brain, especially the right hemisphere, can be directly stimulated through the power of suggestion. As a teaching method, suggestopedia makes particular use of relaxation exercises designed to remove any anxieties on the part of the learner which might act as blocks to learning. The exercises include the use of visual images, music, rhythmic patterns as well as dialogues and translation practice which are undertaken in relaxed and informal settings. No attention is paid to a student's grammatical errors. A main aim is to help learners feel that language learning is a positive and natural process. Great emphasis is placed on creating a reassuring but stimulating environment for language learning. Teachers following Lozanov's suggestopedic methods need to be skilled in singing, acting and psychotherapeutic techniques.

syllabus   A syllabus is an account of the contents of a (language) course and the sequence in which particular content is to be taught. Syllabus design is closely related to curriculum planning (see **curriculum**) for the objectives, methods and testing procedures selected will affect the kind of syllabus constructed. For example, a **grammar–translation** approach will tend to result in a closely specified syllabus of particular structures of grammar and vocabulary. (see also **task-based syllabus**)

syntactic cue   (see **cues**)

syntax   (see **grammar**)

systematic–functional linguistics   (see **functional linguistics**)

systemic–functional grammar   (see **grammar**)

task-based syllabus   The communicative approach to language teaching has led to extensive exploration of the kind of syllabus which will best support it. Some applied linguists have argued that communicative competence is best developed by presenting learners with carefully graded activities or 'tasks'. As the tasks become more complex so they require a more developed set of communicative skills. Thus, a communicative syllabus should not be linguistically graded but be constructed according to the difficulty of the tasks required of the learner at different stages in a course. A task-based syllabus is also sometimes referred to as a procedural syllabus.

TESL   TESL is an acronym for Teaching English as a Second Language. (see **EFL**; **ELT**; **ESL**; **TESOL**)

TESOL   TESOL stands for Teaching English to Speakers of Other Languages. The acronym is also used by a large international organization of teachers and other professionals in the field of second and foreign language education through the medium of English. (see **ELT**; **IATEFL**)

testing / tests   Language testing is a process by which a student's ability, knowledge, performance or progress in language use can be measured. Tests can be diagnostic, providing the teacher with valuable information on which to build lesson plans, and/or evaluative, ranking students according to their ability to achieve specific objectives. In terms of test types, a major distinction is between criterion-referenced tests and norm-referenced tests. In criterion-referenced tests, students have to reach a predetermined level of performance. In norm-referenced tests, students' performance is measured relative to the achievement of other groups of comparable students rather than to an agreed criterion score.

text   This is a term commonly used by linguists to refer to a complete stretch of language, either spoken or written. A one-line advertisement or headline can be a text since it is a complete semantic unit but the practice of text analysis (also known as text linguistics) is not principally concerned with individual words or sentences. It is concerned with the ways in which they combine across sentence boundaries and speaking terms to form coherently organized language in use in a specific context.

Although texts are spoken as well as written, for purposes of analysis the analyst effectively always deals with a written record. It should also be recognized that the term 'text' often refers to a definable communicative unit with a clearly discernible social or cultural function. Thus, a casual conversation, a sermon, a poster, a poem or an advertisement would be referred to as texts. In some studies in this field, the terms text and text analysis can be interchangeable with discourse and discourse analysis. (see also **coherence**; **cohesion**; **discourse**; **discourse analysis**)

top–down (processing)   (see **bottom–up (processing)**)

Total Physical Response   Total Physical Response is a method of language teaching developed by James Asher in which the importance of understanding and acting upon a sequence of instructions is stressed. Particularly in the earliest stages of learning, the language, simple orders, instructions, and commands are given which require action or 'physical response' on the part of the learner, such as opening a door or sitting down. The method stresses the importance of aural comprehension and of learning by doing.

transformational–generative grammar   (see **grammar**)

translation studies Translation is an area within which there is a long history of linguistic applications. Most obviously, linguistic descriptions of different languages and studies in **contrastive rhetoric** are of considerable value to translators. Central to processes of translation is a continuum from free translation to literal translation where much will depend on the translator's judgement of the context, purpose, and audience for the translations. In the case of some literary translations, especially of poetry, there may be no precise formal equivalents and translators may produce a version which seeks to capture the spirit of the original. The value of translation is estimated differently within different cultures; for some it is a menial task, for others it is an intellectual discipline requiring considerable sensitivity to language. (see **culture**; **grammar–translation method**)

verbal deficit (see **deficit hypothesis**)

vocabulary There are several levels to the description of vocabulary. This reflects the multiple functions of vocabulary: words are single items; in partnership with other words, they perform lexical and grammatical functions; and recent studies have demonstrated the important role that vocabulary plays in the formation of complete spoken and written texts.

An important distinction is between 'lexical' words and 'grammatical' words. Grammatical words, as we might expect, belong to a finite set of words with fundamental grammatical jobs to do, that is, mostly pronouns, articles, prepositions, conjunctions, auxiliary and modal verbs (e.g. *they, them, a, an, the, in, to, because, will, must*). Of course, lexical words also have grammatical functions, but they have more lexical content and are (theoretically, at least) an 'open', infinite set, that is, nouns, adjectives, verbs, adverbs (e.g. *castle, bright, walk, contentedly*).

From this broad division, we can see that it is easier to map meanings onto and between lexical words. These relations include traditional categories such as synonymy (words with similar meanings) as well as such categories as hyponymy, where, for example, *vehicle* is an all-embracing superordinate which includes such words as *car*, *bus*, *motorbike*, *lorry* and so on.

Recent work of an applied linguistic kind has stressed that semantic connections between words can operate across and between sentences as well as within individual lexical phrases, sets or categories. Clearly, conjunctions play an important part in such connectivity, but so do other kinds of words. Such words are termed lexical signals. The following made-up sentence neatly encapsulates the kind of text-forming jobs certain words can do and the kinds of signals they can send about how whole texts hang together:

The reason for these occurrences is to be found in certain aspects of the problem.

This sentence does not have much meaning on its own. Words like *reason* or *problem*, *aspects* or *occurrences* signal that there are semantic chains elsewhere in the preceding or following parts of the text into which these words provide hooks. Inherent in the semantics of many words like this is a text-forming function, signalling, as it were, the logic of the text. In order for writers to make a text's structure overt to a reader, they have to learn how to signal appropriately. Some semantic structures in texts are more important than others. Helping learners use words better involves them in using words effectively in complete texts both in first and second or foreign language learning contexts.

Applied linguists have addressed themselves to other aspects of vocabulary and language learning than the description of lexical structure and lexical relations. For example, there have been innumerable studies into the nature of vocabulary learning, particularly the retention of words, that is, why some lexical items are easier to memorize or forget than others. Other studies have examined on what principled bases vocabulary can be selected and sequenced, the role of context in the comprehension of vocabulary and the relationship between vocabulary acquisition and the learning of grammatical structures. After having suffered a period of relative neglect, vocabulary now occupies a key position in the fields of applied linguistics and language teaching (see **coherence; cohesion**).

whole language   (see **holistic; interaction**)